Taxes

By Linda Crotta Brennan

Illustrated by Rowan Barnes-Murphy

The Child's World®

Published by The Child's World®
1980 Lookout Drive • Mankato, MN 56003-1705
800-599-READ • www.childsworld.com

Acknowledgments
The Child's World®: Mary Berendes, Publishing Director
The Design Lab: Design and production
Red Line Editorial: Editorial direction

Design elements: Eric Krouse/Dreamstime

ISBN 9781614732440
LCCN 2012932822

Printed in the United States of America
Mankato, MN
July 2012
PA02122

About the Author

Linda Crotta Brennan has a master's degree in early childhood education. She has taught elementary school and worked in a library. Now, she is a full-time writer. She enjoys learning new things and writing about them. She lives with her husband and goofy golden retriever in Rhode Island. She has three grown daughters.

About the Illustrator

Rowan Barnes-Murphy has created images and characters for children's and adults' books. His drawings have appeared in magazines and newspapers all over the world. He's even drawn for greeting cards and board games. He lives and works in Dorset, in southwest England, and spends time in rural France, where he works in an ancient farmhouse.

Tomás was eager for the woman behind the counter to hand him the double-scoop ice-cream cone. He had his $2 out and was ready to pay. "I'll need 15¢ more," she said, "for the **tax**."

Tomás frowned. "Tax?" He pulled a dime and a nickel from his pocket and handed them to the woman.

"I wish we didn't have to pay taxes," he said.

"My mom says taxes pay for important things people can't pay for by themselves," said Mia.

"That's right," said Tito, Tomás's uncle. "Almost all societies have had taxes. There have been taxes for thousands of years."

Taxes have been charged on all kinds of things. In ancient Egypt, there was a tax on cooking oil. In the 1700s, Russians paid taxes on beards, beehives, boots, chimneys, and drinking water. And around 1800, England began taxing wig powder.

"Taxes pay for things all around us that we see and use every day," explained Uncle Tito.

"Let's look for things taxes pay for on the way to the park," said Mia.

"I found something," said Mia. "Taxes pay for traffic signals."

"And street lights," said Tomás as they waited to cross the street.

"And roads," added Uncle Tito.

A police officer directed traffic.

"Taxes pay for police officers," said Tomás.

"Firefighters, too," added Mia.

"That's right," said Uncle Tito. "You two seem to know a lot about taxes."

"Miss Singh talked to us about them in school," said Mia.

"Miss Singh!" Tomás exclaimed. "Don't taxes help pay her to work as a teacher?"

"They do," said Uncle Tito. "Money from taxes pays for public schools and libraries."

The trio reached the lemonade stand.

"Hey, this park is another thing taxes pay for," said Mia.

"It is," said Uncle Tito.

"That's a lot of stuff," said Tomás. "It's no wonder we have to pay taxes."

"And **federal** taxes pay for things we haven't talked about," said Uncle Tito. "For example, money from federal taxes pays for the postal service and the military."

"What does *federal* mean?" asked Tomás.

Federal **income taxes** pay for many things provided by the US government. This includes Medicare and Social Security. These provide health insurance and money to individuals. Science programs and highways are funded this way, too.

"We have three levels of government: local, state, and federal," explained Uncle Tito. "Cities and towns are the local level. Individual states are the state level. The US government is the federal level."

"And they all collect taxes?" asked Mia.

"They do," said Uncle Tito.

"Local governments usually collect money through **property taxes**," Uncle Tito continued. "These are paid on big things people own, such as houses and cars. And there might be a local **sales tax**. State governments might have a sales tax, too."

"Like on my ice-cream cone?" asked Tomás.

"That's right," said Uncle Tito.

Mr. Smith, the softball coach, passed by on his way to practice. "I heard you talking about taxes," he said. "Some states also have an income tax. The federal government has an income tax. With an income tax, people pay a certain percentage, or part, of the money they earn."

PROPERTY TAXES

Amount due: $1,234.56.

Different types of taxes are collected different ways. Local governments bill property owners for property taxes. Retailers collect sales tax when they make a sale. Federal and state income taxes are usually taken out of an employee's pay.

"Many people think this is the fairest way to tax," Uncle Tito added. "Poorer people pay a lower percentage of tax. Wealthier people pay a higher percentage."

"I've heard my dad talk about income taxes." Mia said. "He said he doesn't like to pay them."

"I don't think anybody likes to pay taxes," said Uncle Tito.

"I think we pay too much," said Mr. Smith. "We should cut taxes."

Uncle Tito frowned and shook his head. "If we cut taxes, we'd have to cut important services that affect many people."

Mr. Smith held up his hand. "Let's not argue," he said. "You make a good point."

"People don't always agree on taxes," added Uncle Tito. "They disagree about how to tax and how to spend money from taxes. Learn as much as you can about taxes. Then, you can make your own decisions about them."

Every year, people who earn a certain amount of money in the United States fill out a **tax return**. It shows how much income tax they owe. If a person paid more than they should have, they will get a **refund** from the government. If they paid too little, they owe the government.

17

"Is it OK not to pay taxes?" asked Mia.

"No. You have to pay taxes," said Uncle Tito. "It's the law."

Tomás scratched his head. "Didn't the Revolutionary War start over unfair taxes?"

"I remember," said Mia. "The colonists didn't want to pay the tax on tea. They dressed up like Native Americans. Then, they threw the tea in the harbor. That was the Boston Tea Party."

April 15 is tax day. This is the deadline for filing federal income tax forms and any money due. Sometimes, the due date changes, such as when April 15 lands on a holiday or the weekend.

"The problem was more than taxes," explained Mr. Smith. "The colonists were taxed without having any say. They had taxes without representation."

"The tax laws were made by Parliament, England's government," added Uncle Tito. "Colonists didn't have any **representatives** in Parliament to speak on their behalf."

Mr. Smith nodded. "Things are different now. We have a say in how we are taxed and in how our taxes are spent."

The Internal Revenue Service, or IRS, collects federal income taxes in the United States. A form of the IRS was first started in the 1860s, during the Civil War. The US government began an income tax to pay for the war. The modern IRS was created in 1953.

Jack rolled up on his skateboard. "Boy, am I glad you're here. I sure am thirsty."

"And I'm glad we have this park," said Mia.

"Me, too," added Tomás. "We have a place to play and to have our lemonade stand."

"Taxes make this possible," said Uncle Tito.

"They sure do," Mia and Tomás agreed.

Glossary

federal (FED-ur-uhl): Federal is having to do with the whole country. Federal taxes pay for the US military.

income tax (IN-kuhm taks): Income tax is money taken from or paid on the money a person earns. Part of Mr. Smith's salary goes to pay federal and state income taxes.

property tax (PRAH-pur-tee taks): This is money paid yearly on something owned, usually a house or car. Mia's dad pays property tax on his house.

refund (REE-fuhnd): A refund is money given back or repaid. Many people get a tax refund each year.

representative (re-pri-ZEN-tuh-tiv): A representative is someone who speaks for others, as in government. American colonists did not have representatives in Parliament.

sales tax (sayls taks): A sales tax is money a customer pays on something in addition to the item's price. Tomás had to pay sales tax on his ice-cream cone.

tax (taks): A tax is money paid by a person or business that supports the city, state, or federal government. We all have to pay taxes.

tax return (taks ri-TURN): A tax return is paperwork filled out each year to determine if income tax is owed to or should be refunded by the government. Mr. Smith files a tax return every year by April 15.

Books

De Capua, Sarah. *Paying Taxes.*
New York: Children's Press, 2002.

Minden, Cecilia. *Understanding Taxes.*
Ann Arbor, Michigan: Cherry Lake,
2009.

Web Sites

Visit our Web site for links about taxes:
childsworld.com/links

*Note to Parents, Teachers, and Librarians:
We routinely verify our Web links to make sure
they are safe and active sites. So encourage
your readers to check them out!*

Index